Contents

Night and day

That night was a dark day. Of course, all nights are dark days, because night is simply a badly lit version of day …

Lemony Snicket, from *The Slippery Slope*

Have you ever wondered why we have day and night? How is it that when some people are having breakfast, somewhere else in the world, others are having dinner?

One of the most important scientific discoveries was about the **rotation** of the Earth and major planets. At any time, half of the Earth faces the Sun and has day while the other half is dark and has night.

Long before scientists were wondering about light and shadow, **Aboriginal People** were passing down stories of the day and the night. In some Asian countries, people were celebrating festivals about the full Moon.

Did you know?
Day and night happen because the Earth rotates on its **axis**. It takes 23 hours, 56 minutes and 4.09 seconds to complete one rotation.

rotation a complete turn
Aboriginal People the first people to live in Australia
axis an imaginary straight line about which something (such as the Earth) spins

While one part of the world gets sunlight, there is always another part of the world that is dark.

LET'S FIND OUT

- What causes daytime and night time?
- What is an eclipse?
- What happens when the Moon gets between the Earth and the Sun?
- Why do people in some Asian countries celebrate the Moon Festival?
- Why is the Moon important?

In our solar system

Imagine you could hold the world in your hands. Some of the world (where your hands are) would be in shadow, and some would be in light. You would have created your own night and day!

The Earth, the Sun and the Moon

The Earth and all the other major planets in our solar system **orbit** the Sun. The Earth also rotates on its axis while it orbits. Just like when you imagined holding the world in your hands – while some of the world is in shadow, the rest is lit by the Sun.

orbit travel around another planet or moon on a regular 'path'

There is also a link between the Sun and the Moon. At night, the Moon **reflects** light from the Sun, like a giant mirror.

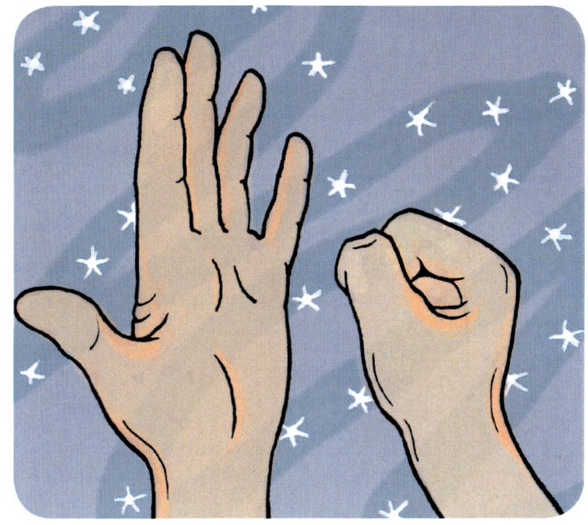

If you hold up your hands, palm to palm, and make two fists (your left fist is the Earth, and your right fist is the Sun), you can pretend light is shining from your Sun-fist onto one side of your Earth-fist.

The Earth is only lit up on the side where the Sun shines on it. The back of your left hand would be shady (night) while your thumb and fingers (lit up by the Sun) would be in daylight.

Luckily, the real Earth spins in space, which is how we have daytime and night time.

---

reflects causes the light to move in a different direction

Breakaway tasks

Remembering

1 In your own words, explain how the major planets move in relation to the Sun.

2 What is reflected by the Moon at night?

Understanding

3 Write a summary explaining how you think day and night happens. You can draw a diagram to help.

4 With a partner, perform the 'Earth-fist' example from the text. Show your class and explain.

Applying

5 Write a short poem about why the Sun and the Moon are both important.

6 Draw a map of the Earth, the Sun and the Moon with arrows to show which way they are moving.

Analysing

7 Make a Venn diagram showing what the Earth and Moon do and don't have in common.

Evaluating

8 What is important about the Earth's orbit around the Sun?

9 What do you think is the most important thing about the rotation of the Earth? Prepare a short speech.

Creating

10 Construct a mobile or a model of the Earth, the Sun and the Moon using resources in your classroom.

The Moon Festival

Chinese Moon Festival

The Moon has been important to people for thousands of years. It has helped people to see and hunt. It has helped sailors to navigate – it has even inspired poets to write!

Moon **festival** celebrations have been held throughout Asia for more than a thousand years. That's a lot of moons! The festival is held on the fifteenth day of the eighth month of the Chinese calendar during the full Moon – that's September or October in Australia.

For Vietnamese and Chinese people, the Moon Festival (also known as the Harvest Festival) is one of the most important celebrations of the year.

festival a day or a few days of celebration

The festival has three traditional meanings:

- gathering (getting together to help with the harvest)
- thanksgiving (for the crops)
- praying (for a good future).

In southern China and Vietnam, the festival is celebrated with dragon and lion dances. Beautiful painted lanterns light up the night.

During the Moon Festival, families make and share **traditional** mooncakes. These cakes are round and made of pastry with a filling of sweet bean paste or **lotus** seed paste. Usually, mooncakes are quite small, but some chefs have been known to make them nearly a metre in **diameter**!

traditional a long-established custom or belief, part of a tradition
lotus a food plant
diameter a straight line passing through the middle of something, such as a circle

Breakaway tasks

Remembering

1 In Australia, when do people celebrate the Moon Festival?

2 Are traditional mooncakes big or small?

Understanding

3 Create a five-question quiz about the Moon Festival and choose a classmate to answer your questions.

4 Give an example of how people celebrate the Moon Festival.

Applying

5 Design a poster about the Moon Festival, based on what you have read in the text. Include illustrations.

6 Find information on the Internet and create an illustrated recipe for traditional mooncakes.

Analysing

7 Create a mind-map showing all the elements of the Moon Festival and how they relate to each other. Use the Internet for your research.

Evaluating

8 List the three most important aspects of the Moon Festival and explain why you chose them.

Creating

9 Design and make a simple paper lantern.

10 Write a poem or a song about a young Chinese or Vietnamese boy or girl attending the Moon Festival.

When the Moon got in the way

The Sun was quite cross with the Moon in the sky,
So she shone her light in the Moon's eye,
The Moon yelled: "Give it a break, eh?"
The Sun replied: "Moon-Face, get out of the way!
I'm trying to shine on the Earth, down below,
All they can see is your great big shadow!"

The Moon stared down at his shadow below,
As it skated across fields, cities and snow,
"I'm terribly sorry, of course, you're quite right;
I didn't mean to put a hole in your light!"
The Sun smiled warmly with her great lips,
As those on Earth enjoyed the **eclipse**.

eclipse when a planet, moon or star is completely or partly hidden by another

Breakaway tasks

Remembering

1 Why was the Sun cross with the Moon?
2 What did the Moon cause on Earth by travelling in front of the Sun?

Understanding

3 Draw a cartoon detailing what is happening in the poem. Write a caption for the cartoon.
4 Create a list of words in the poem that you think are scientific and those that are humorous.

Applying

5 Create a flow chart of events in the poem in the order in which they happened.
6 Rehearse and then perform the poem for your classmates using props in the classroom.

Analysing

7 Do you think the Sun and Moon became friends? Explain.

Evaluating

8 The poem uses humour to describe a solar eclipse. Does the illustration help you understand the poem?

Creating

9 Rewrite the poem into a song and, with a partner, perform your masterpiece for the class.
10 Write an advertisement for an upcoming solar eclipse and explain why people on Earth should enjoy it.

How the Moon got into the sky

This story is from Cape York.

Many years ago, people realised that a light was needed at night time because they found it difficult to walk around or to hunt. The Sun lit up their daytime – something was needed to light up the night.

They held a big meeting and one idea was to collect a huge pile of firewood during the daytime hours and setting fire to it just as the Sun set. People thought that the fire would be big enough to light up the bush so that they could hunt and walk around and have **corroborees**. Most of the people thought that this idea was **impractical**.

One member of the group had a great idea: why not make a special **boomerang** that would shine, throw it high into the sky and at night this boomerang would give enough light to allow people and animals to see at night.

corroborees Aboriginal dance ceremonies
impractical not wise or suitable to do
boomerang Aboriginal hunting tool usually made of curved wood, designed to be thrown

They made a giant boomerang. People tried to throw it high into the sky. They tried but they just couldn't throw it high enough.

Then, a very thin, old, weak man stepped forward and politely asked if he could try.

Everyone laughed at him when they saw his weak, thin arms. One of the elders was a kind and wise man and he said the old man should be allowed to throw the boomerang.

And throw the boomerang the old man did! It went higher and higher and higher, and finally stayed up in the sky as the Moon, shining down onto the people.

The shape of the boomerang can still be seen in the Moon every month.

Breakaway tasks

Remembering

1 Why did people want to light up the bush at night time?

2 Describe the man who threw the boomerang into the sky.

Understanding

3 Draw the Moon and then shade in the shape of the boomerang.

Applying

4 Perform this traditional Aboriginal story in a small group for your class.

Analysing

5 Create a list of everything you *know* about the Moon. What did you learn in the story?

6 Draw a picture of the old man who stepped forward. Why did everyone laugh at him?

Evaluating

7 Why do you think people did not believe the boomerang idea would work?

8 Suggest a different solution to end the story, if the boomerang had not worked.

Creating

9 Create a newspaper article reporting on this story. Choose a photograph to accompany the article.

10 Design your own boomerang.

Strands in action

Core tasks

1 Research some interesting facts about the Sun, the Earth and the Moon. Organise and present these facts to your class.

2 Create a model of the Earth, the Sun and the Moon, showing how eclipses and night and day happen. Make sure you label your model to show what is happening.

Extra tasks

1 Create a mind-map with the Earth in the centre and list everything you have learnt about its relationship to the Moon and the Sun.

2 Use the Internet to research another Aboriginal story about the Sun and the Moon. Choose one to read to your class.

3 Using the Internet, research three major cities in the world, discovering what time it is if it's 12 p.m. where you live. Is it day or night for those cities?

4 Research a different culture from around the world. Include information about their beliefs of the Moon, the Earth and the Sun. Present your research as a poster.

When writing, **paragraphs** are very important to readers and writers. Usually, each paragraph has one main idea and some other information, which helps us understand the main idea better.